CIRCUMVENT CLIMATE DISASTER

DISASTER

The Future Is Now

Seth

Grayson

Copyright

Printed in the United States of America

Contents

Why This Guide?

CIRCUMVENT CLIMATE DISASTER is a book written specifically to make a significant difference by creating awareness and to help sensitize the community and beyond about climate disaster, and the need to solve the problem of climate disaster in the world.

This book is written passionately to express more of the modern ways to navigate through climate change at zero level. In this book, you will find more details, strategies, and solutions with a better approach.   This book is written in chapters to showcase the diverse causes of weather and climate change.

The book highlights the environmental effect of air burn, climate disaster and what to do to put an end to these disasters

About the Author

Seth Grayson is a science enthusiast with over 8 years of experience as a climatologist. He passionately follows and analysis the atmospheric and weather condition. His strength is in figuring out the solution to complex problems. Seth holds a Bachelor's Degree in Applied Climatology and Regional Climatology respectively from MIT, Boston Massachusetts.

Chapter 1

INTRODUCTION

More Clouds

Do you know heat is being trapped in a big car called earth? It might also interest you to know that the effect of climate change is not about rising sea levels, and hotter weather; is more fire, more clouds, more storms, more floods and these effects of climate change can be more deadly and more frequent. In today's world, climate change has become a matter of interest and a lot of people have gone into research on how to avoid climate disasters. Before we deliberate on climate disaster we can first of all break down the meaning of climate.

What Is Climate

Climate is the long-term pattern of weather in an area, typically averaged over 30 years. More rigorously, it is the mean and variability of meteorological variables over a time spanning from months to millions of years. <u>Wikipedia</u>

We could also say that climate is the definition of the weather condition in a specific region over a long time.

Now that we have a clear picture of what climate is, we must relate it to climate disaster

What Is Climate Disaster

Have you imagined a flood covering a whole community? do you think that lives will be spared when fire automatically takes over a district where there are mineral resources that enhances the economy of a nation?

The record shows that the central region of Vietnam experienced a very heavy downpour of rainfall from October 6 2020 that led to flooding in eight provinces. This occurred because of varieties of several weather systems.

Many people loosed properties, some were injured and there was a death record. The record shows that 357 people were either dead or missing, and 876 people were injured. 511,172 houses submerged, 3,429 houses also collapsed, while 333,084 roofs of houses were blown away. In the past 100 years, it is assumed this is the worst storm and flood they have experienced because of its fatalities and the effect.

The experience in Vietnam is a clear example of climate disaster, it can also be described as climate change. This is a situation where the climate is affected by some activities carried out by human being that is capable of distorting the atmospheric composition which could lead to unexpected weather conditions like heavy rainfall.

In the day the sun shines and warms up the surface of the earth and at night the surface of the earth becomes cool and releases heat into the air whereas some heat is trapped in the atmosphere

Some activities humans' beings are involved in can also cause climate change which can result in global warming. Trees help to trap some greenhouse gases in the atmosphere, but when these trees are removed the greenhouse gases is released into the atmosphere all trees or plant whether small or big takes in carbon dioxide and release oxygen into the air when trees are cut down and burnt which could lead to global warming because the carbon dioxide consumed by these plants are now retained in the atmosphere. Forest degradation also cause weather disaster. Natural gas drilling and oil drilling are also activities that can cause climate change because the pollution that goes into the air when burning fossil fuels could lead to climate change and ocean acidification, the major source of carbon pollution is the burning of fossil fuels which also is a major agent that can cause global warming and can also decrease the soil PH which is called acidification. Permafrost is also an agent of climate change as it occurs in areas where the ground temperature is permanently frozen, fertilizers, electricity production, etc.

Are you aware that the atmosphere is increased with 51 billion tons of greenhouse gases yearly, this number has not been constant over the years, it is either more or less but for now this is where we are? This number reduced a bit in 2020 due to the shutdown of industries that was initiated by the Covid-19 pandemic but there was no definite number released in 2020 this makes using fifty-one billion still correct and that we must decrease to zero in the next 30 years to avoid climate disaster.

Chapter 2

WHY ZERO

Zero describes an attempt to reduce the production of greenhouse gas, which is responsible for climate change that must decline to zero to checkmate climate disasters in the near future, climate change poses a great threat because of the amount of carbon dioxide that radiates into the atmosphere. So much attempt has been made to curb the human activities that are responsible for the emission of these gases into the air. There are a lot of ideas on how to reduce carbon dioxide in the atmosphere to zero, some research emphasis planting of trees, Direct Air Capture (DAC) which is an innovation that is already in place in Switzerland, it is a way of sucking the carbon dioxide in the air to reduce its effect.

51 billion greenhouse gases are added to the atmosphere every year, to avoid the threat of global warming, there is a need to get to zero from the 51 billion earlier mentioned. This is so because everything we do as humans starts from what we eat, our movement from one location to another, the things we produce for our comfort all these activities emit greenhouse gases into the atmosphere.

Research shows that the population is increasing rapidly, which in turn suggest that there will be an increase in the demand for food, the movement of human beings will increase and the demand for production by industries will increase as a result it will also skyrocket the rate of greenhouse gas emission if efforts are not put in place to curb the situation.

The need to invest more in research that is capable of inventing a world where everyone can have access to clean energy and electrical movement that will not require fuel fossils so that the agenda to Zero will be achievable.

If we can control some activities humans' perform that have the property of fascinating the infrared that radiates from the Earth's surface and absorbs itself to the Earth's surface again, hence donating to the effect of greenhouse gases. Some examples of greenhouse gases are very vital water vapor, carbon dioxide CO2 is reported to be a very important greenhouse gas that occurs naturally and the activities carried out by humans increase through the burning of chemicals in high temperature that releases smoke and methane. The rate of greenhouse gases can be reduced to zero if we balance the quantity of vapor, smoke, carbon dioxide discharged into the atmosphere from sources where these gases are produced like human activities which consist of synthetic halocarbons and carbon dioxide, greenhouse gases are also produced from Anthropogenic sources like combustion is a process of burning fossils fuels like oil, natural gas, coal that is released when organic matter decay and dissolved itself into the earth, the ocean, and rock.

The production process of electricity and Transportation can aid in the reduction of emitting CO2 into the atmosphere by introducing renewable energy into every sector of transportation, whether land, air, and sea. There are a whole lot of ways the transportation sector can get to zero if the car is made far more efficient in their fuel usage, there could also be innovations like electric cars that can be charged by wind turbines. This is to say we can use these electric cars instead of cars using fuels to reduce the rate of fossils fuels burnt into the atmosphere. Trucks and vans can also be manipulated to use gas instead of or electricity while electric engines can be created for passenger planes to replace Hydraulics and biofuels can take the place of fossil fuels for aircraft.

Agriculture is another great influence that releases greenhouse gases into the atmosphere coupled with waste management and land-use change, industrial activities, and treatment activities. Very huge investment and systematic innovation are required to make technology efficient and supply alternative economic supply that can abate the radiation of the greenhouse gases to meet the Paris agreement target. The Paris Agreement is a treaty on climate binding international change legally. It was adopted by 196 Parties at COP 21 adopted this treaty in Paris, on the 12th of December 2015 and entered into force on the 4th of November 2016. It was targeted at limiting global warming to at least 1.5 degrees Celsius. Greenhouse gases reduction can be achieved by engineered biological remedies like changing land management and planting trees. Nevertheless, these technologies can also have some unfavorable consequences. For example, the United Kingdom is a nation that has given the fight for climate disaster an awesome consideration which has made the emission of CO_2 reduce drastically to 38% since 1990. The major factor tied around the reduction of UK CO2 emission is cleaner electricity that is mixed with gas and renewables that can be used instead of coal, and also the homes, businesses, and industries have reduced their use and demand for energy.

The emission of CO2 has fallen from about 600m tones of CO2 in 1990 to 367m tones in 2017, the reduction in the usage of electricity is based on industrial and residential sectors and they have both reduced their demand to about 25% in 2017. The United Kingdom and international emission accounting practice count bioenergy as zero-carbon when it is used, and they also replaced coal with biomass-fired power.

It is not possible to ignore the limitations and negativity posed by the proposed technological innovations that will be of great advantage to reduce the emission of greenhouse gas, but we still have to proffer some possible solution that can last long and also create an atmosphere where the demand for coal will be drastically reduced and there will be alternative so that the zero aimed out can be achieved.

To achieve zero a lot of innovations need to come in place so that some of the activities we are involved in that are a catalyst of greenhouse gases will be eradicated.

There should be innovation in the energy sector, where pure hydrogen will be burnt to generate power. According to Bill Gates, with hydrogen, energy is extremely powerful, but it has a challenge that might slow the use of hydrogen which is power is also required to extract hydrogen thought a huge investment is put in place all ready for the transition of grey or blue energy.

The transport sector also requires innovations that are capable of transforming its activities into electrical, renewable energies, and battery storage systems. Transiting from fossil fuel will require different green energy alternatives as substitutes, to avoid the large number of carbon dioxide being produced and discharged into the atmosphere.

Chapter 3

NOT SO EASY

There are so many reasons why it will not be easy to transit from 51 billion into zero, these reasons are so clear because it directly affects the populace.

If the price of a commodity is low, there is the possibility of higher demand this makes it a great challenge for some products to be totally eradicated. For example, coal, this product has a great demand because of the comparatively low price to other products, and it is also a difficult task to automatically move human beings from a product they have tested and used to into a new product they perceived to be manageable, this makes it really hard to move people from coal.

There is also a struggle that might be very difficult to conquer if we consider nations whose major source of economic progress depends on oil. How can you convince such a nation to stop the production of fossil fuel? For example, in Saudi Arabia, the production of oil is used for local industry

The reduction of greenhouse gases emitted into the atmosphere that retains heat in the atmosphere is going to be hard to abate hence the ideas to create alternatives to the activities that are responsible for the production of these gases into the atmosphere tends to be bedeviled by a lot of limitations that cannot be easily attended to, for example, the growing number of the world population makes it difficult because the more number of human beings added the higher the number of carbon that radiates into the air.

Some questions will be considered when you talk about climate change that will make it somewhat difficult to achieve the concept of zero. The Quantity Of The 51 Billion

This is a big question that has not gotten a direct answer because the 51 billion yearly is tackled by different organizations that are working steadily to achieve the concept of zero for example the airline that is tackling 17 million tons a year and that is about 0.03 percent of the global emission annually.

Breakthrough Energy Ventures, is an investor that funds technologies that can remove nothing less than 500 million tons a year if their activities are not been altered.

Why Cement

When you consider the nitty-gritty in the process of tackling greenhouse gases and the activities carried out by human beings that is capable of releasing CO2 into the atmosphere you will realize that cement and steel is about 10 percent of the sources of greenhouse gases emission. Recycled materials can be used to reproduce steel and plastic but there is no alternative for cement yet and this poses a great threat to arriving at the proposed zero.

How Much Power Are We Looking At

This is a vital issue as it affects power generation directly, for example, New York has 12 gigawatts even though the seasons and time determine the figure while Tokyo has way more population than New York requires about 23 gigawatts and might need more because of the rate of her population. What is the possibility of providing solar panels that can produce this much gigawatt to suffice for the amount required to supply the population enough power needed by the populace?

How Much Space Do You Need

If we emphasize the use of nuclear power we require space where the equipment will be kept, if you intend to generate electricity with the wind in the place of solar, a lot of space will also be required to achieve this.

How Much Is This Going To Cost

The price to pay to reduce the emission of greenhouse gases is expensive because if you consider moving from dirty fuel to green premiums that are carbon-free the difference is about 600% more expensive which makes it difficult.

The heat trapped in the earth tends to change the balance in the energy the earth receives from the sun that reradiates into the earth being a major source of climate change responsible for global warming. It will be very difficult because the advantages of CO2 are enormous and it is going to be difficult to eradicate.

So many countries are economically dependent on oil and gas and might not be in support of eradicating the use of fossil fuels, because of its benefit to their economy they will negotiate the idea of reduction of greenhouse gases so that their economic advantage won't be blocked.

Chapter 4

WHAT TO ASK IN EVERY CLIMATE CONVERSATION

Bill Gates in his research on climate disaster, highlighted five questions that can be asked in every climate conversation.

How We Plug In

Plugging intends to describe how we use electricity and its effect on the climate, it is recorded that if we can produce natural light with wind, sun which is the solar system, this will reduce the fossil fuel generated from burning gas into the atmosphere in an attempt to produce light.

The generation of power supply is about the highest source of carbon dioxide emission; research shows in the United States 57% of the energy used in power generation goes through the coal burning process which is capable of producing a high percentage of carbon dioxide (CO_2) compared to other sources that generate power like oil and natural gas. There are Some other sources of electricity production that don't produce carbon dioxide or a little amount of carbon dioxide, like nuclear systems, wind, solar, hydropower, etc. another method of power supply generated from crops waste, livestock waste, power plants, methane, etc. radiates carbon dioxide into the atmosphere but may not contribute to global warming because they are also involved in the prevention of methane and carbon dioxide.

How We Make Things

Factories and industries have played a major role in some damage the environment has encountered, the fact has it that 2/3 of the greenhouse gases that caused climate change emanated from these sectors.

The toxic and unpleasant materials that radiate into the atmosphere does not only put the planet's ecosystem a great risk but are also responsible for some health hazards.

Factories are not the only generators of pollution that affect the climate negatively, but they are the primary source of greenhouse gases. So much effort is required to correct the process of production in factories and some industries so that the generation of these dangerous pollutants can be checked.

The toxic materials and some gases burnt and exposed to the atmosphere like methane and carbon dioxide are some of the agents that resulted in global warming. Global warming is not a pleasant situation as it can lead to a lot of unpleasant situations like an increase in Tsunami, hurricanes, floods, rise in sea level, rising earth temperature, melting of ice caps, extinction of some species of animals.

A combination of the toxic generated from industrial factories and automobiles tends to increase the risk of developing some health-related challenges like lung cancer, heart disease, chronic respiratory disease, and many more. Our wildlife has suffered a great negative effect as a result of this pollution and a lot of species have gone into extinction.

Water pollution has also been a subject of interest as a lot of factories dump their contaminated water, chemicals, gases, toxic waste, into the seas and ocean thereby causing damage to marine life.

The pollution of the soil has made some land unproductive and infertile as a result of the industrial waste being deposited into the land, the chemicals have destroyed some areas and have left some land fallow without anyone to till the soil because the condition of the land cannot be ascertained because of the continuous deposit of toxic materials.

So many people lost their lives as a result of air, water, soil pollution, etc. the world health organization recorded that about 5% of patients diagnosed with lungs cancer, lungs disease, chest infection, heart disease, etc. will be credited to long time exposure to the different pollution sighted above.

The quest for natural resources like oil, wood, coal poses a great danger to the ecosystem, trees are cut down to get wood for building structures and another construction process, while causing a lot of our wildlife to go into extinction, miners also eject animals from their place of comfort just to achieve their aim.

Oil spillage is also another concept that has left so many species into extinction and the hope of the situation ending soon cannot be ascertained.

The process of production can contribute positively or negatively to the reduction of greenhouse gases released into the atmosphere from 51 billion tons to zero there is a recommendation that using recycled materials in producing new products can be of great advantage in radiating gases into the atmosphere and are also cheaper to produce, this can only apply to things like plastic, and steel but there is still no alternative for cement yet.

How We Grow Things

Farming releases a good number of methane and nitrous oxide, which are two threatening greenhouse gases. Methane is produced during the process of digestion by livestock, it could also escape out of organic waste or manure stored.

The greenhouse gases emission from the land use act, agricultural practices, land clearing, and forestry is being recorded as up to 22% of the greenhouse gas emission experienced in the world, it amounts to 29% if fertilizer transportation, sales, and processing are included. Climate change is affecting land globally, temperature is rising over land at about twice the normal rate of the original global temperature, this has intensified the heatwaves, rainfall, and flooding globally. Drought has increased in dryland by about 40% since 1961. Productivity in agriculture has been greatly reduced in so many regions like Australia. These climate changes can also lead to loss of vegetation, permafrost, fire damage, biodiversity, soil degradation, and coastal degradation.

This can cause water scarcity and reduce the supply of food and this can be highly influenced by high population growth, the response of every community, and the consumption style.

Farmed animals are also considered a major source of greenhouse gases which makes it advisable to adopt plant-based diets. The research report shows that about 25-30 percent of global food production is wasted, if this is not controlled it can as well increase the rate of greenhouse gases emission.

When the forest is used for another purpose, the carbon dioxide stored inside the forest will be released into the atmosphere. Land plays a very important role when we talk about the 51 billion tons of greenhouse gases released into the atmosphere, the land has the capacity to both absorb and release the greenhouse gases into the atmosphere.

This also implies that land has both advantages and disadvantages when we talk about climate change challenge As we all know plants inhale carbon dioxide during the day and release oxygen through photosynthesis, biologists grow plants like soybeans, rice, and wheat inside greenhouses where they supply the plants with extra CO_2 to make it grow well, recently "Free-air concentration enrichment is experimented by some scientist in the world where these crops grow in open fields and carbon dioxide is supplied to the plants through some pipes. The release of this CO_2 can lead to climate disaster if not checked.

Getting Around

Carbon dioxide and other greenhouse gases like methane, hydrofluorocarbons, methane, and nitrous oxide are produced when we burn fossil fuels any time we use diesel and gasoline in the transportation process, it warms up the atmosphere and can result in climate change. Research shows that 29% of greenhouse gases are released in the United States and it is the highest contributor of greenhouse gases.

How We Stay Warm And Cool

Using air conditioners to keep cool or hot or using your refrigerators is another source that produces greenhouse gases called hydrofluorocarbons, while these gadgets keep our homes, cars, and offices cool, they increase the cause of global warming and hydrofluorocarbons are capable of damaging the ozone layer.

Chapter 5

WARMER WORLD

Climate disaster used to be a subject discussed but now it is a reality that everyone in the world is a part of and is being affected by global warming. As the environment is getting warmer the earth is bound to experience unpleasant weather conditions. Since the 19th century, the rate at which temperature is increasing is been alarming and there is nothing we can do about it, the average temperature annually is estimated to be about 4.5 – 9 degrees and the rise in sea level has also risen and it's now between 8 – 20, there are weather forecaster predicting storm and flood. The government, individuals, and businesses need more information on the current weather condition so they can be more prepared for what they stand to experience in the near future. Efforts are being made to curb this menace that is expected in the future if global warming is not tackled in the right direction but most data provided isn't accurate and inadequate.

The government should direct investment towards adaptation-centered research because solutions are required in various areas like food productions and human health. The question is how do we prepare to adapt to this warmer world. "Manning says, "As people experience more effects of climate change, we're going to have to work towards finding ways to lift people out of more grief and trauma. We may have to go into a methodized state"

People are being affected in one way or the other by the effect of global warming, according to Bill Gates as a result of the rise in sea levels and change in floodplains, everyone has to rethink the locations we erect our homes and offices and plant more trees that can trap the carbon dioxide that has been released into the air by some human practices.

This isn't a situation where individuals can do so much, but more responsibility is laid on the government to invest in making the world adaptable for her citizens by investing into carbon dioxide equivalent to reduce the release of greenhouse gases into the atmosphere.

Chapter 6

WHY GOVERNMENT POLICIES MATTER

Government policy is very important when it comes to the fight against climate disaster because it is a policy that will aid the activities of every responsible citizen in a nation. Making these policies will help to restrict some human activities that might be detrimental to the climate.

The Government is expected to make policies that can guide and restrict the ecosystem. This will make people have regard for nature like the Ocean, mangrove, forest, rivers, etc.

The Government can also support small agricultural producers who show interest in the restoration of the land use act.

If the government can promote green energy to diversify the burning of fossil fuel and make clean energy a priority to the populace

'Tackle the heat already caused by the release of CO2 into the atmosphere Government need to give grants and incentives to business owners to improve the efficiency of energy and conserve it.

Government can enact policies that will encourage advanced research that can drive clean energy technologies.

Congress can pass laws that are capable of regulating and funding programs that will sensitive the populace and encourage the Clean Air Act.

Chapter 7

PLANS FOR ZERO LEVEL

Every year, it is recorded that 51 billion tons of greenhouse gases is added to the atmosphere which has become a threatening situation globally. If strategies are not put in place to checkmate the emission of these gases into the atmosphere in the next 30 years, the earth might become difficult to live on because of the consequences of the pollutants that are been released into the atmosphere that is capable of causing global warming.

These gases increase every day in larger amounts because practically everything we do as human beings influences the production of greenhouse gases

Bill Gates in his book admitted that" the very idea that one person is saying they know what we should do--- but this technical know-how has some limitations that are capable of obstructing the potency of the structures. He says "The world is not exactly lacking rich men with big ideas about what other people should do, or who think technology can fix any problem" but making this challenge a priority is the greatest impediment on the path of the breakthrough of this course.

To make progress in the fight against climate disaster Bill Gates and his team initiated a term called "Green Premium" he said Green Premium is meant to differentiate between the cost of a product or a process that emits carbon and the one that does not.

Green Premium could not thrive in the passenger car sector to an extent where people can conveniently afford cars. Bill Gates went further to say that tech innovation is good and required at this point to curb the threat of climate disaster but any tech innovation that is initiated from the united states or any other part of the world must be made affordable for people who live in countries like India to be able to purchase it.

The radiation of greenhouse gases can be reduced to zero in 2050 when renewables are used to generate power. For example, small-scale wind generation, solar panels on the top roof, solar water heating, geothermal energy, fuel cells that can be powered by natural gas, and renewable hydrogen.

The main strategies adopted to get to zero are

Migrating to electricity and other greener fuel, increasing the energy efficiency, taking advantage of natural techniques to eliminate the carbon in the atmosphere.

We should be able to judge if the clean energy source is good

1. How much power or land is needed in generating energy because you have the equipment and plant to store and how consistent can this produce energy.

2. How many people die being involved in the whole energy value change, so many people die in coal mining compared to the nuclear energy industry.

Energy production should be redirected to nuclear waste production. The nuclear plant is efficient in terms of how much materials are needed, though nuclear energy isn't perfect it has to be encouraged and find a way of making the nuclear waste safer and cheaper and also reduce the technical barriers.

3. Another way is sucking out carbon from the expensive atmosphere, even if we get the price down to $100 per ton of carbon dioxide removed, 51 billion tons of carbon emission globally per year will cost 5.1trillion dollars and the other challenge is Direct Air Capture (DAC) can only remove carbon dioxide from the air and cannot remove methane and nitrous oxide

4. Green premiums this is a way to think about the gap that needs to be closed between dirty options and clean zero-carbon options for example shipping companies use bunker fuel which is cheap and dirty, a gallon of bunker fuel cost 29 cents compared to electro fuel and alternative which is greener and clean which is $9.05 per gallon this is almost 600% difference

Bill Gates answered so many questions on the reduction of greenhouse gases and he said trees can lock in carbons, provide shades, green a place; so planting a tree can be a way of getting to zero.

According to Kaskeala, the net-zero target is a framework that can be misused, this makes it important to emphasize the minimization and reduction of emission and carbon radiation. He also emphasizes that compensation should be a useful tool to approach the target zero and to be carbon negative.

Chapter 9

ACTION CORNER

Each and everyone should take action and be committed to reducing greenhouse gases to checkmate global warming. Our target is carbon dioxide is an enemy of climate and it is released whenever fossil fuels, oil, and coal are burnt and to get energy in an attempt to power our electrical gadgets, we can be committed to contributing our quota to avoiding global warming and also saving money.

As a person OR individual take it as your responsibility to be involved in the fight against global warming, if efforts are combined and directed towards this singular goal a great result will be achieved take for instance in New Zealand about half of the greenhouse gases produced there is produced from agriculture compared to other sectors like manufacturing, power, transport, etc. research shows that reduction of our intake of meat and dairy and a shift to agricultural products that is rich in protein and also rearing pets that feed on more on a plant than animals. can be a bold step toward the fight against greenhouse gases.

As humans or an individual, if we decide to appreciate locally produced food to avoid the danger of carbon being discharged into the air while ships and flights go about importing food from nation to nation. Research shows that goods transported from one nation to another are responsible for 3.3% of global carbon dioxide (CO2) radiation and 33% of fossil fuel combustion is also from this same source.

The use of cars could be minimized to reduce the discharge of carbon dioxide (CO2) into the atmosphere, alternatives like bicycles and public transportation should be a better option, take for example a city of about three million people using their cars at the same time, the level of carbon dioxide that will be released into the atmosphere at that time, this poses a great danger that can be avoided if we all put our hands on deck to achieve a common goal. Having this knowledge will provoke the idea of using an electric bike that could be very effective and fast compared to normal bicycling.

Trees are of great advantage when we consider the fight against global warming. Naturally, plants produce their food through a process called photosynthesis, they take in carbon dioxide and release oxygen, if we can plant a tree every day as a person, this can go a long way in checkmating the effect of greenhouse gases that is become a treat globally. Trees have a great advantage apart from being able to receive a good amount of carbon dioxide discharged into the atmosphere, it makes the environment green, it reduces the effect of wind on the environment.

In this journey, trying so hard to avert the effect of greenhouse gases reduced into the atmosphere, if a clear decision can be made by individuals who travel by air to improvise alternatives to their scheduled journeys by reducing the number of times air transportation is utilized. There could be options like using zoom, creating internet conferencing, and having branches in different locations so that the need to travel on air will be minimized.

As an individual, if you're connected to the government of your nation or if you are a politician, there is a need to invest in climate awareness programs that will enlighten the populace on the need to be climate-conscious and the possible risk involved if the level of greenhouse gases released into the atmosphere is not checked and what every person can do individually to avoid the dangers. This can be taken as a great project for lovers of the world, for example, Bill Gates is a one-man who has taken the fight against climate disaster as a project and has even written a book to that effect so that a lot of people who might be so busy to listen to the news might also have time to read a book on climate advocating the dangers of delay in fighting the course of global warming.

It is also very important that if we leave this fight to politicians alone, we might not be able to achieve an excellent result because if we compare the percentage of politicians in every country of the world it is little and a lot of them do not have climate as their priority when coming into office, so a lot of times they take the fight against global warming secondary forgetting the implication if not tackled fast and smart. This is to say as an individual, fighting climate disaster should be taken as a priority to have many hands attacking this future menace where unpleasant conditions can be averted.

Chapter 10

CLIMATE CHANGE AND COVID-19

Covid-19 is a pandemic that committed great havoc in the last few years, economies were slowed down, so many people lost their lives, some lost friends, family members, husbands, wives, children, and jobs. Whenever you mention Covid-19 the first thing that comes to mind is an era of trouble, interestingly, this pandemic was an advantage to the environment, as you know, borders were shut down, this made a lot of people remain in their homes and countries, Air travels were put on hold, in most places sea and land travels also had restrictions which made the world had a standstill. As a result of the pandemic, a lot of people were kept indoors, Airlines were shut down like some other parastatals of every nation; this made the carbon dioxide emission reduced drastically. Air pollution was reduced as a result of the work from home system adopted during the covid-19 pandemic era.

Steven Davis who is a professor in the department of Earth system science at the University of California said 500 tons of carbon dioxide (CO2) per $1 million of the world GDP in 2019, 40 billion tons of CO2 were emitted per $88 billion of the world GDP. This shows that if Covid-19 persisted, the world GDP might be able to have a reduction in global carbon dioxide emission.

The Director of the Global Energy Center, Randolph Bell also in his findings said Atlantic Council that the recession that was experienced by the economies was connected to the covid-19 virus and it caused a drop by 25% in the lockdown of four weeks.

Any activity that affects human being will also affect the environment, in China's Stanford University, Marshall Burke of the department of Earth science states that if we create a functional economic system that supports people without threatening the earth there won't be any reason to query if the virus was good or bad for the economy.

In a nutshell, the virus was a threat globally but an object of reduction of greenhouse gas emission.

REFERENCES

AIDA

UN climate change report

Breakthrough Energy.org